REI BOUNTIFUL
A Collection of Poetry

Pamela K. Yarborough

outskirts
press

Render Me Bountiful
A Collection of Poetry
All Rights Reserved.
Copyright © 2023 Pamela K. Yarborough
v5.0, r1.1

This is a work of poeticized fiction. The opinions expressed in this manuscript are solely the opinions of the author and do not represent the opinions or thoughts of the publisher. The author has represented and warranted full ownership and/or legal right to publish all the materials in this book.

This book may not be reproduced, transmitted, or stored in whole or in part by any means, including graphic, electronic, or mechanical without the express written consent of the publisher except in the case of brief quotations embodied in critical articles and reviews.

Outskirts Press, Inc.
http://www.outskirtspress.com

ISBN: 978-1-9772-6042-0

Library of Congress Control Number: 2023902432

Cover Photo © 2023 www.gettyimages.com. All rights reserved - used with permission.

Outskirts Press and the "OP" logo are trademarks belonging to Outskirts Press, Inc.

PRINTED IN THE UNITED STATES OF AMERICA

*For anyone who has gone to find their
mother after years of longing for
her gentle touch and sweet embrace.*

Contents

PREFACE — I

RHAPSODY — 1

   SUN KISS — 2
   SIMPLE PLEASURES — 3
   THE SLOPING TREE — 4
   TRUE HAPPINESS — 5
   MEMORIES — 6
   MINE TO KEEP — 7
   COZY CLOUDS — 8
   GOODBYE TO SUMMER — 9
   IMPRESSIONS — 10
   A LITTLE BIRDIE TOLD ME SO — 11
   NOT READY FOR SPRING — 12
   FOR BEAUTY'S SAKE — 13
   OH, MUSIC! — 14
   A PLACE TO BEGIN — 15
   ECLIPSED PERFECTION — 16
   SUMMER IN JUNE — 17
   AUGUST NIGHT — 18
   BUTTERFLY — 19
   SHADES OF AUTUMN — 20

STARS AND DUST — 21

   BATHE IN YOUR SWEETNESS — 22
   BLUE MORNING — 23

YOUR EYES	24
YESTERDAY, TODAY	25
THE REEL WORLD	26
YOUR GIFTED HANDS	27
A TOUR DE FORCE	28
BEAUTIFUL THING	29
AM I REALLY SURE?	30
PIMPLES AND DIMPLES	31
CONFESSION	32
YOUR FAVORITE FLOWER	33
HEAVEN KNOWS WHY	34
AT TWENTY YEARS	35
AN ARTIST'S DUTY	36
HOURS IN A DAY	37
LUV BUG	38
IMAGINE YOUR SMILE	39
SOMEONE ELSE'S DREAMS	40
LOVE'S RETREAT	41
HEARTS FOREVER YOUNG	42
JUST FINE	43
I REMEMBER WHEN	44
WITH LOVE	45
HELLOS AND GOODBYES	46
SOMEHOW I UNDERSTAND	47
MAGIC LIGHT	48
FOREVER BLUE	49
TRACES OF YOU	50
AFTER WINNING	51
IN THE MIDDLE OF A DREAM	52
A LOYAL FRIEND	53

TENDERNESS YOU'VE YET TO FIND	54
SPLIT	55
THE LAST POEM	56
WHEN YOU'RE GONE	57
SWEET SURRENDER	58
STEADY WATCHING	59
LOVE IS	60
SMART AMBITION	61
SOMEDAY	62
ON MY WAY TO MANILA	63
MOTHERS ARE TEACHERS, TOO	64
PERFECT NEVER	65
TO BE LIKE YOU	66
THE PARK	67
LUMINESCENCE	68
NATURE	69
MAYBE IN MAY	70
MY MOTHER, MY FRIEND	71
LABYRINTH	**72**
SO FAR TO GO	73
MAKIN' TIME	74
THINGS WILL BECOME CLEARER	75
OUR MOTHER'S DAUGHTERS	76
FOR MY MOTHER	77
BLACK JESUS, WHITE JESUS	78
THE RACE QUESTION	79
A BRIGHTER TOMORROW	80
THE PANDEMIC	81
PEACE FOR HOURS	82

SONGBIRD	83
THE MAN IN THE MIRROR	84
WE'RE ALL COMPLEX	85
MAY WE SURVIVE THE HOLIDAYS	86
NO GUILT	87
EVERYONE'S SOLD	88
I AM DONE	89
ACKNOWLEDGMENTS	90

"… He drums a beat inside my ear
so clear a sound it's Love I hear."

— E. L. Henry, "By His Voice I'm Lifted"
(*Blue Summer Moon Anthology*)

Preface

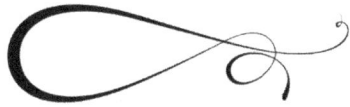

Have you ever lost or misplaced something and was not sure exactly where it was or what happened to it? How about hiding a secret password or an expensive piece of jewelry and then forgetting where you hid it? Who has that not happened to? What is absolutely worse is when you throw away something of great or of sentimental value, and for the very life of you, can't believe you would ever do such an idiotic thing. To say I haven't done that more than twice would not be telling you the truth. What happened with my sister pertains more to the former than to the latter and most certainly pertains at this moment to her phenomenal poetry collection that is now safe and permanently installed, thankfully, within the pages of this most precious book.

I remember days upon days my sister asking, "Where are my poems?" I had no idea to which poems she was referring. I knew of about 10-12 poems that were indeed so wonderful that I wanted to feature them in my anthology of short stories, plays, and poetry published, originally, in 2013 with a revised edition released in 2017, but beyond that I was clueless. She didn't want her poems featured in my anthology, by the way, never giving me an outright reason. I could only surmise it had may have had something to do with splitting

royalties, something she didn't trust would work out. On the other hand, she may have actually believed that somehow she would get cheated, entirely, out of her rightful share, which I knew that if that did occur, it would have had nothing to do with me because I wanted her to always have everything, even more than what I had managed to acquire for myself in all my working days and years. So, here I was not thinking too much more about her "lost" poems when I, unknowingly, during a discussion about the ones missing, said something not to hurt her feelings in any way but because I desperately wanted her to focus solely on the poems I knew, and with utmost certainty, she had indeed written. The ones I happened to be already in possession of, and I could assure her, at any moment, that I knew exactly where I had placed them. With this said, it saddens me that I made, when looking back, a comment based not on any fact whatsoever. "You don't have enough poems for a book," I abruptly said. I recall her not responding to my absurd comment (although I didn't know how absurd at the time), and instead of acknowledging my comment in any way, she stared off into space and walked toward the brown recliner to sit where she, typically, sat day after day when lounging in her living room. It was after she passed away that I knew what that far off look meant. It meant that one day, with God as my witness, we would find her vast collection, and then the joke would be on me, the one who hadn't been clever enough to piece together the puzzle, the one who could never, ever find the lost or missing poems, despite how hard and desperately I searched before finally giving up altogether. I couldn't be totally blamed because for years I lived away either while attending school or

traveling or working and had no idea that her poetry had not only blossomed into pure greatness but was put away (away, away), and as secrets go, the whereabouts were never shared with me. When I returned back to Maryland to reside permanently, I did find it necessary to provide my sister with a variety of storage options, including the use of file folders for the purpose of securing or keeping organized her important papers, mail, etc., but none of these items were good enough to meet her needs, especially when her main objective was to hide away certain papers (and poems, too!) that, regrettably, and later to both our dismay, remained hidden, God knows for how many days, months, or years, from even her. Nevertheless, her expression on that day told me everything I needed to know but only I didn't, at the time, know it. And that is, after journeying home to heaven on the day God requested her presence before Him, there, with all respect still given to the omnipotent, holy, and divine one, she would be, yes, smiling to herself, maybe laughing a little, too, over the mystery solved regarding the poems neither she nor I ever found when she was here.

On a sunny afternoon in mid-August shortly following my sister's passing, my cousin, Roxane, and I were in her apartment sorting and packing many of her things. Roxane (Praise be to our Holy Father!) was her industrious, as ever, self. After a time of doing this and doing that, she pulled from inside a neatly covered basket a plastic bag from behind my sister's brown recliner. Again, the same one she sat in every, every day. I asked Roxane to hand me the bag. There

was something suspicious about the ordinary white plastic bag, and I felt an urgent need to take a quick peek inside. Why would her precious poetry be in this bag? It was almost immediately that I knew what my sister's intentions were. She wanted to fool would-be thieves into thinking there was likely nothing of any value inside. Unfortunately, I was fooled also, the one who really needed to know. Just as I mentioned in the beginning, here was a prime example of hiding something and soon forgetting where you hid it. When looking inside the bag, I noticed a slew of folded papers, folded over four times exactly, I would later find, each and every one of them. This was to further discourage any would-be thief from being even slightly interested if discovered. Now, there was no obvious clue as to how important or unimportant these folded papers were, but I instinctively knew (Thank God I did!!) I had better take this bag home and look over each separate and folded piece one by one. When I did arrive home and got settled, still not sitting down as yet, I opened the bag and noticed that on each and every piece of folded paper pulled from inside was one single, illustrious poem. I did not sit down and could not sit until I completed reading every poem, which, after counting each one, totaled an astonishing one hundred and eleven. To say I was mesmerized is putting it mildly. Throughout the hour or more of my standing and reading non-stop, I could feel nothing but enormous pride, happiness, sadness, and regret all rolled into one. My regret centered mainly on not being able to celebrate the wondrous moment with my beloved sister because she was no longer here on Earth to rejoice in discovering what she had, for so many years, held so dear.

Still, I was over the moon with happiness. She had, beyond my deepest, deepest wishes, left for me her greatest gift, her beautiful heart and soul planted firmly and forever in each one of her poems. I imagined her writing with a pen in her right hand or typing as she did with only a few, and as odd as it may seem, though not to everyone, there she was on each piece of paper still with me, still talking to me, still in the present with me, and still beside me. I was given a miracle and was in a bit of shock at how blessed I was and how grateful I was that God placed Roxane with me on that fateful day to fulfill a purpose that He commanded be completed, which was to find my sister's missing poetry that wasn't really missing or lost as we now know. He knew where they were, and He knew after all the years that had come and gone, they would be found on that very day. I am in awe, to this day, of that moment happening and decided right then I would take charge of leaving for my sister a most valuable and enduring legacy. I would commit strongly to getting right to work no matter what it took or however long it took. I would remain steadfast and stay more determined than ever to publish her very own incredibly outstanding and, needless to say, long overdue collection of poems that were better than any I had either studied or had read in a very long time. I selected eighty-six for this publication and these poems, her best ever ones, are to forever honor her memory, her gifts, and her being referred to, in time, all due to her amazing collection, as a poet supreme. For anyone reading her poetry can plainly see how the wonder of God existed inside of her, not once diminishing or fading over her entire lifetime. But rest assured that I don't ever need a book of hers or a special occasion to

do what comes so naturally for me to do every day. I honor my dear and sweet Pamela, my twin, my love, each day and night in my prayers, in my thoughts, and in my heart. I smile when thinking how she was so regal at times, so much so that I told her, more than once, more than twice, that in a past life, she must have been either very rich or a reigning queen and I, her highly devoted servant or subject because she demanded (and nothing less!) sacrifice, honor, and, most of all, undying and unselfish love. That's what she wanted, and that's what I was happy and most willing to give her to the very end of time if I could. After all, God gives us the most precious of these things, undying love, the very moment we are born. Wouldn't it make sense then that I and everyone should aspire to be just like Him? Who was I to not try my very best at giving her all that was given to us so freely by our devoted and heavenly Father?

Publishing my sister's book is what is expected of me. When I hear His call, I answer. When I see His truth, I tell it. When He tells me to move, I move.

Patricia K. Yarborough

Rhapsody

SUN KISS

Here in this place
While the wind
It warms my face.
The moon I want to chase
Here on this hill.
My senses I want to fill.
Here the stars heighten
My awareness that I'm
A living being
And that beauty is so freeing.
The night shines as
The world unwinds.
Colors fade to black until
The day comes back to
Welcome the world to
The morning's glow; to
The sun we've come to know;
To the kiss she bestows upon
Us each day; to the debts
We owe her.
I pray she shines her glory
Upon us as she lights
Our way.

SIMPLE PLEASURES

Simple pleasures of a rainbow
That I treasure.
Umbrellas dotted along the beach –
Melons, plums, and a big, juicy peach.
Marvelous is how I feel, and summer
Clouds I wish to steal.

Echoes of thunder, storms of wonder –
Rest your mind –
Try to find some time to kill.
Maybe daydream upon a hill.

THE SLOPING TREE

The sloping tree does not stand
Straight and tall and looks as if
It's about to fall.

It must have been injured in a
Storm because indeed it's not
Perfectly formed.
It looks a little out of place
Sort of like a black sheep among
Some families that didn't grow
Up quite so normally.

Still I love that crooked, old tree
Cause it stands out among the rest.
And to me it's the best because
Its leaves still sway whenever there's
A gentle wind.

What's more it can better protect two
Lovers from the harsh summer sun
And maybe be a refuge for someone
Who's just completed a long, hard run.

TRUE HAPPINESS

Summer's gone, and autumn is thrust
Upon us shedding its leaves of gold.
Reveries pass from tales of old telling
Shoots of spring to bud its fold.

But soon ahead there'll be enough
Preparing for festive holidays
Filled with caring… signs of wispy
Snowflakes fondly asking to not
Forget the years when happiness
Meant winter was near.

And me? I'm just waiting for the day when
The world will stay one beating heart,
One illumined mind.

A day we'll be having one grand time.
A day of true happiness I hope to find.

RENDER ME BOUNTIFUL

MEMORIES

I listen with my heart when
Hearing a song telling me of the
Softness of snowflakes that linger
Surprised in my hand.

I remember those warm melodies
During the cold, coldest of winters
When my eyes could see the
Faintest green on the barren trees.

MINE TO KEEP

As I awakened, the sun
Was breaking up the night
In pastel colors so bright it
Formed a crystal dawn
Right before my eyes.

A breeze was blowing
Making me feel at ease
Knowing that as the sun
Sets, one by one counted
Are dreams I won't forget
And for a lifetime stay kept
As my very precious own.

RENDER ME BOUNTIFUL

COZY CLOUDS

Hide within the softness
Of a cloud
When the noise
Becomes too loud.
Behind a safe space –
Fortress spun from
Splayed sun rays happy
There is nowhere else
For me to run.

GOODBYE TO SUMMER

Let's say goodbye to warm weather
But not forever; goodbye to sunny skies
And fireflies; to the warm ocean that seems
Forever in motion; to sandy beaches and
Smooth, ripe peaches.
And as the leaves turn a reddish brown and
Fall silently to the ground, I'll be thinking of
Snowflakes dreaming by the fireplace and
Looking to November for the warmth that I
Remember.
As I say goodbye to summer, and the old oak tree
I daydream under, I welcome winter with
Hope and wonder.

IMPRESSIONS

Season of change
Perfection of a lily –
Roses for you, silly!

Impressions of the sun
Newness of spring, and
Winter is done.
Grass will be green, oh,
What a lovely scene,
And boy, will we think
Wasn't winter mean?

Thoughts of you under
A cedar tree.
Irresistible weather for
Birds of a feather.
Misty mornings, and come
What may, the lazy days
We'll wile away.

The earth is where
You'll find me planting
Flowers that burst into
Bloom from April showers.

RHAPSODY

A LITTLE BIRDIE TOLD ME SO

Splitter, splatter
You ask, "What's the matter?"
Rain is falling from the sky, and
You have to wonder why.

Look down, there on the ground
Raindrops slop, flop…the sound
You hear.
Then the drops, they disappear.

Have you ever asked what makes
The clouds thunder, or the
Reflection, refraction of sunlight
Through falling mist?
That's what a rainbow is.

The same deal with a sunbow.
Do you know how I know?

A little birdie told me so.

NOT READY FOR SPRING

I'm not ready for spring.
It all seems too soon, and
I am just not ready for spring
And that sort of thing.

Spring cleaning… I get that special
Meaning of new beginnings, but I'm
Sad for winter's ending.
I'm just not ready for spring and that
Sort of thing.

I cannot deny the beauty of hearing a bird
Sing or the lovely daffodil, my favorite
Flower if you will.
The warm spring breeze –
It's all a summer tease.

The leaves have turned green, and from
What I've seen, spring has arrived,
And nature is alive.
Still I miss the snowflakes for
Goodness sake.

You see, I'm just not ready for spring and
That sort of thing.

FOR BEAUTY'S SAKE

There once was a man who
Desired nothing but to
Live alone in the forest.
He would shun civilization to
Become one of the poorest.
Said he wouldn't miss the city.
Thought it wasn't very pretty.

He would sit by the lake and cry for
Beauty's sake when counting each and
Every star.
He wouldn't miss the sounds
Of fast cars and noisy bars.
He refused to suffer others' moods
And their often unpleasant or
Unpredictable attitudes.

Dying to sleep under the vast and starry
Sky, he would, for beauty's sake, ask
Over and over, "Why, why, why?"

OH, MUSIC!

Oh, music, the countless ways I listen with
My eyes.
No new trick to see a song when I watch the
Sunrise.
I listen with my nose to a tune like the perfume
Of a spring rose.
I listen with my hands when I hear a
Song about the softness of a touch when the
Day has turned to dusk.

I listen with my voice when I hear a song that
Screams and shouts.
I sing out loud and rejoice.
Alas, I listen with my ears to music so dear to
Sounds of the flute –
Sustenance, like fruit, that brings so much cheer.

Oh, yes, it's all so sentimental,
And did I mention?
Imagination is instrumental.

RHAPSODY

A PLACE TO BEGIN

Beautiful summer, what have you done?
You've brought me the warmth of the sun,
But no one to love, which is what I
Mostly dream of.

You have blessed me with rainbows and
The stars that glow, and while that's reason
To sing, there's no love for me it brings.

As autumn comes around, and as the leaves
Clutter the ground, I'll think of it not as the
End but as a place to begin.

ECLIPSED PERFECTION

The trees loom against a perfect sky.
Birds sing melodies when dancing by;
Ever higher they soar in flight –
What a glorious sight!
Below children fly a kite in the
Darkening daylight hoping to
Not settle quickly into the
Warm summer night.

RHAPSODY

SUMMER IN JUNE

It's summer in June, and my
Heart like a flower will bloom.
My senses will awaken to the
Fresh morning air, and I'll
Pretend I haven't a care.

Gone is the winter chill when up
Pops a daffodil, and even though
I love the sound of snowflakes falling,
I'd rather hear the songbirds calling.

It's summer in June.
I pass away the hours pressing
My face into flowers on a
Long and lazy afternoon.
I sit with my back straight against
A friendly tree and stuff myself
Wild with blackberries.

So, pardon me if I don't seem
Too much in a hurry.
It's summer.
I'm a child again, and life is
Oh, so, merry.

AUGUST NIGHT

Listening to the sounds of an August
Night – the whisper of a gentle wind,
The soft brushing of summer leaves,
Twinkling stars, and thinking
Of what might have been.
A cricket's call to a friend.
The moon distant, unreachable
Playing peek-a-boo when
Another day is at an end.

BUTTERFLY

Tall ivory towers, meteorite showers –
Amazed at the powers of the
Magical butterfly;
Amazed at the colors that blaze
Even when the sky is gray – I am safe
Under my umbrella with this mystical
Fella catching him ever so softly
In my hand and tell myself
Nature's no toy, and to feel freedom
Is to feel pure joy.

SHADES OF AUTUMN

Tall trees that touch the sky –
Hazy shades of autumn
Pass me by.
Above September clouds
Cover headlights beaming at
Twilight.
Islands of people gazing at stars
Gleaming after midnight.
Who'll miss summer?
I think I might,
But in spite of it all,
I'm glad it's fall.

Stars and Dust

BATHE IN YOUR SWEETNESS

I want to bathe in your sweetness –
A heart so blessed.
I want to bask in your glow –
Learn how you know how to
Soothe my woes.

When you smile, I'm happy
For a while.
As I awaken with you beside me
Knowing together there's
No reason to hide.

A sign from the light of
Our deepest wishes –
When we stumble then flee
Into the shining beacon
That will guide us.

BLUE MORNING

On a blue morning winter came,
And like you and me,
Nothing would stay the same.
You said we would rediscover
Each other's love in sweet rapture.
A thousand splendid moments
In our hearts we would capture.

RENDER ME BOUNTIFUL

YOUR EYES

Life's a tease, and your love is
One fine release – In other words,
You set me free.
That's all I ever want to be
Because your eyes, my dear,
Could calm the sea.

YESTERDAY, TODAY

Yesterday, you had the whole world
Wrapped around your man-sized finger.
And today, your bright, red balloon slipped
Away, and all you could do was sigh since
Now it's both you and I chasing it and time
Trying to make our mad reasons rhyme, but
I say it's fine to stop climbing ladders never
Reaching for what is…"I love you."
For in our world, when does saying this
Really or even matter?

THE REEL WORLD

My world is a fairy tale.
Where everything is cotton candy.
Where everything stays fine and dandy.
Where Hope hops aboard my carousel.

YOUR GIFTED HANDS

If I had a choice I'd take the sky
Up above with its sunlit turquoise.
A common bond between you
And me that wasn't there before.

But if I dare to toss miles away
What may be love, better you try
To catch it using both your strong
And gifted hands.

Find a tall trumpet vase to place it in.
Eight red and white roses with the
Prickliest stems at your command.

A TOUR DE FORCE

Cherries are sweet of course,
Beautiful of course.
By the window, cherries in a bowl
On a lace-covered table ancient old.
A knife to slice a piece of pie for you
And for me.
Your cherry pies a tour de force.
"Don't forget the ice cream!" I scream.

Last night, I dreamed of a cherry ocean
In the sky, and can you guess why?
My thanks for the scrumptious cherry,
Dark-sweetened dreams that never once
Tasted of your wily, romantic schemes.

BEAUTIFUL THING

My anger has receded into a pool
Of white water.
Danger has fallen away, away,
Away on this curious day.

Angels have lifted me high, high
Above the ground –
High above the treetops where
A bird sits with eyes like black pearls.

I hear the sound of your plaintive cries
Of how your heart is still bound.
Look around, stand down as the
Rain drops, as the sun lights up the sky.

Please know you will have peace.
You will have love and all the beautiful
Things you can think of long before
Your life is done completely.

You will have won.

RENDER ME BOUNTIFUL

AM I REALLY SURE?

It's ten p.m. as I wait for him to rid
This blight on such a cold November night.
My tender heart will not put up a fight.

Yesterday, I do not regret, but is he up to
The task of making me forget?
Let's not mention the ring, or
Did I say, "Bling"?

Oh, here he comes now.
He knows what's up.
His heart like a cup will catch my tears.
And my world will be sound, and all
Around peace will abound.

But once he's far past beyond my door,
Which part was left for me to be sure?

PIMPLES AND DIMPLES

I remember pimples, and when
Love seemed so simple
And you with one dimple.
Now I've grown into heaven
Knows what with nothing to
Call my own except the stirring grass –
A sound only the wind can
Hear – my only friend.
Having no direction, accepting
Rejection –
Won't you please come
And give me some direction?
Maybe things might take on a
Different complexion.

CONFESSION

Blue sky and apple pie makes me wonder
Why I would never leave you.
Don't know what I'm looking for, but
I'll know when I have found it or it
Finds me… maybe up a tree it will
Envelope me, and my heart will show
No regrets… only the sound of our
Joined melody, and yes, I must confess
That even with less I am blessed.

YOUR FAVORITE FLOWER

Paisley printed dresses; black long
Twirled tresses – daises sprouting
Up from the ground finding
It over at last, but wasn't it a blast
We knew wouldn't last.
In the spring, I'll blossom again
Into your favorite flower and recall
Our quiet tumble in the fall and
Discover I do miss you after all.

RENDER ME BOUNTIFUL

HEAVEN KNOWS WHY

Heaven knows why love shines greener
Than two leaves… A fine belief in you and me.
Blue as the sky is heaven knows why love is,
Too, like a thief, hiding thin under a
Tortoise's armor my long, lost friend in the
Summer always running fast toward the end.

AT TWENTY YEARS

Drowning in my fears at twenty years of
The many promises I may never keep.
When I close my eyes to sleep, dreams are
Never complete…needing someone to
Hold my hand – to tell me a story of hope.
Why is my life on the borderline, and why
Is my mind like a piece of deserted land
Where I'm drowning where I stand?
Closing my ears so not to hear the haunted
Voices, the terrible screams, after years of
Wanting to someday dry my tears…wanting
Something called "Happiness" –
To find out what it means.

AN ARTIST'S DUTY

Finding chiffon pleasures in violet treasures
I measure some of life's forevers in a baby's
Breath – your creative depth, creamy pearls
In a hue of colors that swirl.
Most of all, when I hear your song, I belong
In a world filled with your beauty, an artist's
Duty to bring me such joy when I've been
Deprived of love that never arrived.
Constantly, I strive for the planet Mars, and
The so very distant stars!

HOURS IN A DAY

As we wile away the hours
Touch gently my face, and
Let your lips be still.
Fall in love with the symphonies
To be played, the strings to be
Strung winding tight our two
Separate hearts into one.

RENDER ME BOUNTIFUL

LUV BUG

A sensation to the imagination.
A brilliant star in the constellation.
More than sublime fascination could,
If ever, ruin this infatuation.

IMAGINE YOUR SMILE

The day is done, and the night
Has come as crickets call to
The early fall.

This season of crimson and gold
I dread the impending cold.
I snuggle in my bed and watch
The moon aglow and wish I
Could send it to you wrapped
Up neatly in a bow.

Imagine your smile at such a gift
Received – that to know you are
Loved … is to be believed.

RENDER ME BOUNTIFUL

SOMEONE ELSE'S DREAMS

Days without you, dreams without you is
All I have left since you went away.
The only memories are remnants of a once
Love clutching fiercely at my pride –
Admitting you were only along for the ride.
I guess I got caught up in my own dreams, and
Yours didn't quite include me.
I wanted a true companion, but now my
Heart is as hollow as the Grand Canyon.

LOVE'S RETREAT

Here in the dark with a silence so clear
My distant heartbeat is all I hear.
Aloneness and a longing so strong
I may, out of the blue, just disappear.
With hardly much to tell, retreat into my
Fractured shell …
To glimpse the borrowed light that
Seeps in tempted often to stay
But decides to only sometime dwell.

RENDER ME BOUNTIFUL

HEARTS FOREVER YOUNG

Her eyes are sad because of dreams lost
And roads never crossed.
Her heart is light as a butterfly and often
As needy as a baby's cry.
She believes in second chances and
Wild romances in a world different
From when, as a young girl, dancing was
A lift and a spin with her one and true only.
And though she may get lonely facing
Each coming but still uncertain day, her
Heart plays on a song yet to be sung, a song
Played only for hearts that are forever young.

JUST FINE

Lost in thoughts of dreams I hastily
Bought was taking the easy way out.
You taught me how to rid the awful
Pain I had fought – how to feel like the
World was mine along with the sunshine.
Even though my heart was on the line,
It's because of you I survived just fine.

I REMEMBER WHEN

I remember when you said goodbye, and
I wondered why.
I never put up a fight… I just remember
At night us holding each other.
I was so naïve thinking then you
Would never leave.
I thought we could have gone the
Distance with neither one of us giving
Any resistance.
I'm now left so out of place wondering
If there's a space out there… somewhere
In someone's heart… for me.

WITH LOVE

I knew our love had died, so
I wrote down these words –
That someday in some quiet moment
They will put you at ease.
But never mind the you and
Me that never came to be, or ask why
It was you who floated out to sea.

HELLOS AND GOODBYES

Hellos, goodbyes, frills and lace – your pretty
Face to fill that empty space in my heart.
If we ever part, I'll march in the parade of
Lovers lost – frightened over games we played –
Unparalleled to the love we made.

Sending you best wishes from our lovers' nest.
You know the rest… I loved you best.

SOMEHOW I UNDERSTAND

Ghostly ancestors huddle around me
Speaking in a foreign language that
Somehow I understand as love.

"Oh! Crazy!" you shout.
Barely amazed am I at your doubt.
Just another day here on planet Earth
Where we search to find value in
What we're worth.

But what if love is not found here?
Will we recognize it when it appears?
Would it make us happy or build in us fear?
Do we have this "love" inside us to speak of?

Someday… Someday… Someday…
When we are all ready, we will know.

MAGIC LIGHT

My days are so dark, so dark, but
My nights you fill with your magic light.
You are my nocturnal dove fashioned
From the same crescent moon above.

Where are you during days when my
Pretty words are never heard?
But won't you come until the morning
Sun crosses the lawn?
Then we'll fly away, two bereft doves
High, high above the dawn.

FOREVER BLUE

Days ago, but not so long ago,
I loved you only I didn't know
I loved you, and the comfort of
Your touch I'll never get to show
You just how much I want it to be
True that you'll want... with me the
Same sky so blue.
Forever blue am I without you.

RENDER ME BOUNTIFUL

TRACES OF YOU

Traces of you as bold as the
Midnight sky with juice
From anxious fruit on a
Tongue bathed in kisses.
Falling fast honeysuckle
Rose into the valley below
We flowed.

AFTER WINNING

After winning you, I took one
Deep breath and thought for
What it was worth, we gave birth
To a love as sure as I am standing
Purring like a kitten because
I'm one hundred percent smitten.

RENDER ME BOUNTIFUL

IN THE MIDDLE OF A DREAM

Roses are red, and the sky wintergreen blue.
Gazing at a waterfall when I shew away
A cat's call, but only a dream this is.
Only a dream wishes your melodies
Stay sweet and still cling to me like the
Hot summer heat.

A LOYAL FRIEND

Spring has come for our eyes to behold
Waves as bold as lovers kneeling by
The seashore wanting nothing more
Than to be loved forever as the
Golden sun hovers above them like a
Giant, triumphant, and loyal friend.

RENDER ME BOUNTIFUL

TENDERNESS YOU'VE YET TO FIND

Tell me a story of the secrets in your mind, of
The loves you left behind, of the tenderness
You've yet to find.
Tell me of the night that made you confess all the
Loneliness you've longed to forget.

The cloudiness of that morning; the leftover dreams
From the night you slept; the silent tears you wept.
Your heartbeat is warning you that the day has only
Begun, and the sun may light your way through
One more lonely day.

You stare out your window and see a family – one man,
One woman, and one child laughing so happily.
How you want to be as carefree – not just a shadow on
The wall waiting for the rain to fall.

Who holds the key to the love you seek?
Whose heart will soon open up to speak?

Let this story end with me as your friend.
Leave loneliness flying unfettered into the wind
High over the treetops that bend.

SPLIT

I feel split down the middle, and it hurts
More than a little bit.
I thought you'd be around to keep the
Fires lit, but now there's a hole in my heart
From it being torn wide apart.
I wish I could climb right out of my skin and
Trust somehow that it's not the end – that our
Colors do, in fact, blend.

I thought you'd be around to help me keep
My feet on the ground and my head out the
Clouds where the thunder is so loud.

Strangely, when we meet in my dreams,
It is not as bad as it seems.

RENDER ME BOUNTIFUL

THE LAST POEM

Every poem I write I believe it's my last
Until I think of you with eyes so wise.
I think of the sunset on the day we met,
And all the promises we haven't made yet.

When I was falling like a parachute out
Of the sky, you came along.
I didn't ask why or how you heard me
Calling or how the sunlight peeked
Through the clouds when you said
Right out loud, "I love you."

Is this the last poem I'll write?
Who's to say that when I look out
On some moonlit, starry night or
Gaze out upon the ocean so blue that I
Won't know exactly what to do.

WHEN YOU'RE GONE

You ask what will I do when you're gone.
First, I'll cry, and then I'll go on like before –
Lie awake like any other morning and think
What may be far too many thoughts of you.

I'll go to work and think of you…
I'll paint pastels and think of you…
I'll sit very still and think of you…
I'll look up at the stars and think of you…
I'll even laugh and think of you…

But most of all, I will dream and dream and
Dream of only, only you.

SWEET SURRENDER

It is a lovely springtime here and good
To know you won't be alone because
It is springtime there, too.
You have the warmth from the sun to
Remember the days you were once mine.
It was from May through December when it
Was to your sweetness I surrendered.

STEADY WATCHING

My heart is my voice.
It cries out loud in
A crowd hearing not a sound.
My heart has eyes to see the
Beauty in you that is happy
And so unapologetically free.
My heart is further wise enough
To see the truth in a lie.
A time when my heart says goodbye.
My heart is rich, my
Pockets poor, so I keep steady
Watch at its open door.
My heart has a mind that
Questions any answers I find
Warning me love is often too unkind.

LOVE IS

Love is a big open sky and just you and I,
And never asking why
We fly so high.

Love is fragile as glass like a cool breeze
That may leave
Just as fast.

Love is being with you on a rainy
Sunday and waking with you
On a sunshiny Monday.

Love is that look in your eyes that
are so wise. A whisper in your ear
Just because you are near.

Love's color is a rainbow
Because you made it so.

SMART AMBITION

Ambitious heart
The sky is a work of art.
The stars are twinkling, but
My heart is sinking because
You and I are apart.

Ambitious heart
Don't get too high.
Don't hope too much
For love and such.

Love is for the chosen
Few, but what am
I supposed to do when my heart
Sings for you?

Ambitious heart
Let me be smart to consider this.
With only one kiss my world is
Filled with bliss.

And what would I say if you walked away?
Your tender touch I would long for and miss.

RENDER ME BOUNTIFUL

SOMEDAY

Somewhere on some distant shore
You'll love me like you tried before.
We'll play the game of who is to blame –
Wondering why it's not the same and
Discover passion in mediocre fashion
Lying hand in hand with our backs
Hard against the sand.

ON MY WAY TO MANILA

On my way to Manila, I'll explore the history
Of mystery, find your secret door, and time
Travel as I unravel.
I'll retire at twilight, sleep until daylight, and
With a willow as my pillow find Manila right
At the center of my axilla.

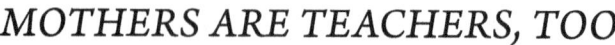

MOTHERS ARE TEACHERS, TOO

Mothers are God sent.
We can place no one above her.
Mothers are also very wise, and
Instinctively know why
A baby cries.

Mothers are tough, and when
The waters get rough, they will gently
Touch your face and tell you that
There's always a place inside their
Heart just for you.

Mothers are teachers, too.
They teach you not just how to sew,
To cook, or how to read a book,
They will set you in search of your dreams
Where in God's unfailing light,
You will find a life that beams.

PERFECT NEVER

There's a perfect time,
A perfect wine,
A perfect day, but there's
No perfect way to say
I love you.

There's a perfect flower for
The perfect hour when near.
The sky so crystal clear…
A perfect time to say
I love you.

A perfect song I hum along.
With you is where I belong.
A mistake if I should ever
Start to love you.

But take this to heart –
My perfect love –
A perfect me I'll never be.

RENDER ME BOUNTIFUL

TO BE LIKE YOU

With his carte blanche, he's
So nonchalant in his rocket
He'll launch to see what
My ordinary soul can
Never behold... so, I'll
Rub two coins between
Both hands, and with
Lots of luck, try harder to
Understand his faraway
Distance if I can.

THE PARK

It's time for springtime dreaming
As we search for meaning in
Echoes of a winter we remember.

Vibrant are our hearts sitting
In the park listening to
The sounds of the meadowlark.

I snap a picture of you in
The color maze underneath
The sun's gaze drinking
Lemonade freshly made.

A lovely day is here
With hearts unafraid.
I present to you roses…
To you I hold so dear.

LUMINESCENCE

On one unreachable star, I will plant a seed to sow
My heart... become luminescent flowers with
Worlds of endless rivers never ceasing to flow.
Where, when standing upon this silvery star,
You can watch me glow from wherever you are.

NATURE

Gazing at some of nature's wonders –
Mysterious, luxurious, rolling streams
Resting in a mountain's pocket, and all
I have to do is dream of moonbeams.

The sky sits in a brilliant ball of fire.
Oh, but I have to more than admire how,
In the end, it's you that my heart requires.

For not even a rainbow can compete because
My darling and dearest you are just as unique.

MAYBE IN MAY

I was so scared because I remember
When no one cared, and at love
I didn't dare.
So, hold my hand along the way, or
Is it too late to smell roses anyway?
They say tis good to pray –
That there's nothing that God
Won't do His way.

MY MOTHER, MY FRIEND

My mother is my friend.
I do intend to repay her for all
That she's done, and even though
She asks for nothing in return,
I give her my love because that's
What she's made of.

Labyrinth

SO FAR TO GO

There are those among us who won't ever
Trust, and there are those who believe
Love is a must.

Those who feel we are owed
When someone steps on our toes.
Those who carry to their graves
Hurts that they never forgave.

There are those who live and let live –
Who forget how to give.
Whose hearts are asleep, and whose greatest
Losses could make the strongest weep.

Let it be said starting from long, long ago
That with God right among us, we still
Have so very far to go.

RENDER ME BOUNTIFUL

MAKIN' TIME

There's so much I want to see and
So much I want to do and
So much I want to be
That sometimes I don't
Have time for thee.

But then I think, what would
I do if you did not have time
For me?

So, I get down on my knees
And pray that you will always
Be there to guide the way.

LABYRINTH

THINGS WILL BECOME CLEARER

I've lost my way.
I can't exactly say how, but
Surely one day I will navigate
This winding road and find
My way back home.

I will feel the wind softly blowing,
Look in the mirror showing a
World slowly becoming familiar
To the face I have missed and have
Long wanted to once again know.

OUR MOTHER'S DAUGHTERS

Trying to find an answer was like trying to cure cancer.
Not so pure, so sure like, let's say, when everything seemed
Like child's play – I remember my sister.
She had her way and, oh, how I miss her.
How the sun seemed to kiss her when we were our mother's
Daughters – who could have, if she were here, taught her.
Too caught was I in a world where no lessons could
Ever reach me, teach me how to be free – how to be me.

FOR MY MOTHER

For my mother, absent from my dreams…
Just yesterday it seems.
Forty years gone, what does it mean?

For my mother who I miss –
Hell, it's been many times I
Fell and crossed many lines.

Stood up only to be knocked right back down.
"Never give up!" was my failed mantra.
Any happy moments were just sheer luck.

For my mother, who I long to kiss.
Such a vain wish…a bliss I'll never, ever know.
The silence of her laugh, the aching inside
Looking at her worn and faintly torn photograph.

BLACK JESUS, WHITE JESUS

What color is Jesus?
Dark as the color of night or white as the
Bright daylight.

Do children know the true color of Jesus,
And could it mean a child may really lead
Us someday?
Would it free us all to love one another as
Sister and brother?

Is Jesus tan like sand or blue as the sky
In some people's eyes, or is Jesus all the colors
Of the rainbow?
Is this all part of some divine plan that no one
Can ever know?

Until we step up to shake His hand, we may
Never understand why it was His color that
Divided the land.

THE RACE QUESTION

Used to be the darker you are, you
Won't go far, but as our flag unfurls,
A Black man leads the free world.
We earned the right to choose –
Lessons learned in the fight for equity
While lies stay to remind us of inequity.
For those who say we won't win, just beat it.
The race question we'll die trying to defeat it.

RENDER ME BOUNTIFUL

A BRIGHTER TOMORROW

A state of mind is blackness, but most
Times I feel the color blue, which I can profess
Even to you.

A Black man is Head of State.
Black Diaspora, we wait as others hate.
The tide is rising to set sail our ships and find
Our shores.
Tis in God we trust, but he's just a mortal man.
That much we understand.
Many questions we ask of this man.
We pray for knowledge from this man.

We stand and walk forward toward a brighter
Tomorrow…unchaining the last of our
Imprisoned sorrows.

LABYRINTH

THE PANDEMIC

Are we in the clear from this past year?
A collective "Whew!" from the lucky few
Who made it through.
We've lost so much losing loved ones
And such.

We cope with mountains of fear and
Whispers of hope we hold so dear.
Angels with gifts of vaccines –
What does this all mean for a future
We dream?

We are not the others who can't walk
The new path we will one day discover.
We are us –grateful sisters and brothers
Who need one another.

Let us live and love…me and you because
This is what we are meant to do.

RENDER ME BOUNTIFUL

PEACE FOR HOURS

Oceans of people are crying.
The greedy have contempt for the needy.
People suffer and orphans are lost without
Their mother.
The land I live in … do I love her … this
America?
Sometimes, sometimes she shines.
At times she's blind.
Let us not be silent when we witness
Her violence.
Cease the bigotry, the poverty, and
On that possibility – we might agree.
Love one another, and don't hate me.
One day you may see me in a
Different light and decide to give up
Your fight.
The wedge between us can no longer
Be an excuse for your power.
Instead allow an array of peacefulness
To last over an abundance of hours.

SONGBIRD

With your bow
And your arrow
You use me
As a wall
Between you
And the
World.

Listen to the song
Of the
Sparrow.
Put away
Your bow
And your arrow.

You'll see
The path to
Freedom
Isn't all that
Narrow.

RENDER ME BOUNTIFUL

THE MAN IN THE MIRROR

Starting with the man in the mirror...
Your face you did erase.
Did you feel out of place as you
Went from brown to white in the
Darkness – in the absence of light?
Did you misplace your soul?
Was it so easy to steal away?
Frankly, it's hard for anyone
But you to say.

LABYRINTH

WE'RE ALL COMPLEX

Who are you calling dense?
I possess plenty of sense.
My mental acumen is not
At all dim.

Oh, wise one! Oh, oracle!
Size me up.
Assess my mental agility.
Find I do have a quantity
Of mental ability in this
Beautiful, capable, and
Awesome mind.

RENDER ME BOUNTIFUL

MAY WE SURVIVE THE HOLIDAYS

Oooh…ghosts, goblins, and witches.
Halloween is here, and I love it.
I'm no pre-teen, and long are those years gone,
But a mouthful of candy corn, and I'm reborn.

Roasted turkey, pumpkin pie, cranberries,
And you know the rest. Thanksgiving for
His grace is next.
What is this I hear? More shopping to
Do where?

Allow me to first savor my delectable
Turkey feast before I muse upon night
After night my many wishes for
A tasty Christmas delight.

With a kiss and songs of prayer, may we
Survive the holidays with a bounty of
Goodness to share.

NO GUILT

A sweet concoction – the best ice cream,
Tutti frutti, so nice and gooey.
In no time do I take to dig my spoon in,
Wrap my tongue around the creaminess,
Too, of my favorite hot fudge sundae I
Want for all eternity.
A hope laden with vanity but not the kind
Most possess.
A cone you suggest.
Maybe that would be best.
Lips colliding with the cherry on top I grin
Endless to begin with.
No guilt ever, if I'm a little fatter.
Long after I'm real old it doesn't matter even
If it's cake batter or real vanilla bean with
Chocolate hazelnuts layered in between.

RENDER ME BOUNTIFUL

EVERYONE'S SOLD

You wear turquoise with much poise.
You wear yellow, and we rejoice.
You're a wonder in green and gold.
Everyone's sold, but don't wear beige.
It just shows your age.
Red reveals your passion for revelry, but
In violet, you are the unequivocal pilot.

I AM DONE

I can say this and mean it.
That a man is as complex
As a grain of sand.
The metamorphosis of
The butterfly.
Tell me why no one knows
The mystery of life.
Figure it is strife to bend
Your mind, to outstretch any lines.
I say forget this one query inside
My mind because for the
Moment, I am done with
Searching blind.

Acknowledgments

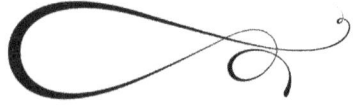

Thank you, precious and mighty Father, for blessing my most dearly beloved twin sister, Pamela K. Yarborough, with her special gift for writing incredibly beautiful, thoughtful, imaginative, and heartfelt poetry. Thank you, too, precious Father, for blessing me with having her in my life for as long as she could stay and for giving me both the will and the determination to publish what is her final gift to us all – an astounding poetry collection. I will love my sister forever as she also loved and showed me the same.

I will be eternally grateful to my cousin, Roxane Alston, for finding what was later determined to be my sister's "treasure trove" of poetry. Had it not been for her consistent selfless and unrelenting care demonstrated when helping me sort through many of my sister's personal and timeless possessions, all one hundred and eleven poems might have been lost forever.

Regina Ewing, thank you for the thoughtfulness when intently listening whenever I asked for an opinion or just needed to be heard. Your kind patience and support I'll remember always.

Thank you to my devoted and dear sister, Sharon McKeever, for the genuine support and love she offered me straight from her heart and for believing, without one single doubt, that she was and will always be a part of us.

My deepest gratitude to Author Representative, Rebecca Andreas, for her unending patience and tireless commitment throughout what could be described often as a fate-filled journey surrounding the publishing of my sister's book. If I wanted perfection, she was right there to assure me it was possible. There were times when it seemed she was, in fact, me, looking through my eyes, feeling inside my soul, and knowing as surely as I did how much this book meant to me. In other words, there's no questioning how far above and beyond my expectations Rebecca did go in allowing me the freedom to have the book published exactly how I envisioned it becoming and keeping always in mind what my beloved and darling sister, Pamela, so often wished for and wanted as well.

My most sincere thanks to the interior designer whose artistic vision captured the essence of what I wanted the book's interior to look like only I didn't have, in the beginning, the words to describe it. The interior designer amazingly channeled whatever it was I couldn't quite express in words and placed it on nearly every page – conceptual and visually inspiring art that I was left speechless when I first saw it – the nature my sister loved, the love she prayed in earnest she would find each day, and on the final page, a beautiful butterfly in flight to remind us all that my sister, the amazing poet that she was, and her most precious dreams, will live on and on and on.

CPSIA information can be obtained
at www.ICGtesting.com
Printed in the USA
BVHW030301120423
662126BV00007B/358